MANIPULATION

The ultimate guide to using manipulation

to your advantage.

Oliver Bennet

Table of Contents

Chapter 1: Laws of Manipulation

Manipulators respond to one, two, or more tactics to reach their aims, always at someone else's expense. While the strategies may vary from manipulator to manipulator, there are 13 manipulative laws each manipulator uses at one time or another:

Law #1 - Hide Your Intentions. Lying may be the oldest and most effective manipulative form around. Manipulators often respond to this strategy when trying to avoid responsibility or twist the truth. Some manipulators also admit to lies where there is no particular justification to do so, only living on the joy of causing confusion or knowing that they play with someone else's emotions. A talented manipulator knows how to operate so subtly on this angle that you don't even realize the lie they are spinning until it's too late. There may be various reasons why a manipulator needs to resort to telling lies. It could be another to take advantage of. To hide their true intentions, so that you do not know what they are up to. Or maybe even to level out the playing field so they can stay a point ahead of you.

Law #2 - Attention Seeking. A little excitement in existence makes things exciting but chaos occurs all too much for a manipulator. Why? For what? And they set it up intentionally. Manipulators want to be the center of focus for validating themselves and offering their egos the boost of trust they feel they deserve. A friend at work may have recourse to generating friction among colleague A and colleague B by sharing tales about each other. This guarantees that while colleagues A or B are at odds with one another, they transform to a manipulator for "comfort," making the manipulator look special afterward. One person may continuously pick a conflict in a partnership to ensure that the other's energy is consistently centered on them and attempting to fix an issue that does not exist.

Law #3 - Behaving Emotionally. Manipulators may be individuals who are extremely emotional, prone to sensational, and even hysterical rantings whenever they want stuff accomplished their way. Overly dramatic, rude, offensive, over-the-top, a manipulator can revert to irrational actions even at the smallest provocation, which is unacceptable in a social environment. A pair fighting aggressively in the cafeteria when one spouse is acting unreasonably because things are not handled their way resort to this action, thinking that their spouse will feel humiliated sufficiently to cede to their requests allows this an incredibly successful coercion tactic when employed correctly.

Law #4 - Playing Victim. Everybody always feels bad. They appear to have the world's toughest luck. Any issue you might have, they search a way of making you feel bad for even thinking about that by finding out how "10 times worse" their issue is than yours. Now and again we all profit from a bit of bad luck; however, the manipulator has learned to use that unfortunate streak skillfully to raise their own "victim" status and to place themselves above all others. A buddy who is continually bringing up all the bad elements of his life when ignoring the problems will resort to this cynical technique to get the publicity they seek. Tell them you've got a rough day since you've had a flat tire on the drive to work the next morning and they'll remind you how fortunate you could still have a vehicle to worry about because they're trying to suffer the public transit difficulties. This emotionally exhausting technique is used by manipulators to receive support from people, that is another means of getting publicity and ensuring that all is centered on them.

Law #5 - Taking Credit Where It's Not Due. Manipulators don't hesitate to get you to do all of the legwork, and afterward, swoop in at the last moment to take credit as they did the lion's job. A common tactic that is often used in a skilled setting, normally in group or team-work projects. Such crafty manipulators are fluttering around delegating tasks, apparently "busy" when they don't do much at all, however, when it comes to claiming credit, they have no problem brushing you back and demanding credit for the innovations and the effort you've put into it.

Law #6 - Depend on Me. Manipulators want you, in your life, to feel like you need them. That you just can't live without them. They are the "popular" ones in a social setting to which everybody seems to flock, making you anxious to want to become a part of that community. They might be the partner in a relationship that keeps reminding you "what you would do without me" or "how you would survive without me." They do you favor and assist you out at a moment when you need it the most, going to make you feel deeply in debt to them so that at a later date they can come as well as cash in on those favors.

Law #7 - Selective Honesty. Have you ever felt so enchanted by how a generous person you know could unexpectedly turn around and stab you back? Or felt so wrong-footed when you recognized you only knew half of what was going on? That's because the person who was feeding you with data was a manipulator, and the reason you feel stabbed in the back or wrong-footed is that they only fed you information that they wanted you to know while intentionally withholding the rest. Selective honesty, a controlling manipulative tactic that can be used to charm an unsuspecting "victim".

Law #8 - Pretending to Be A "Friend". Don't be deceived by the exceedingly pleasant person you merely met at the office on your first day. They might claim to be your buddy while collecting information regarding you to use to everyone's advantage later on. While some individuals may be genuinely friendly, if this individual is a little too pleasant, start raising the red flag by posing very specific or inquiring questions, especially if you've just met them. Inside a professional environment, this technique is popular and if your gut tells you something wrong, it's off.

Law #9 - Non-Committal. Do you know whoever has a hard time willing to commit to anything in your life? Even after you told them how essential it is and just now you could use their support? The non-committal person is not your mate, they are a manipulator. They find delight in withholding their authorization or support if it means they have a chance to give themselves the advantage to control the situation to their advantage. They just look out for themselves and especially deter from contributing to something if it involves taking liability. Being non-committal is a tactic of manipulation which is often used in romantic relations. When a romantic partner is non-committal, it helps keep the other on their feet and keeps them coming back for even more, thus giving the upper hand to the manipulator. The longer they withhold their dedication, the more you will be willing to bend backward, just to get their approval.

Law #10 - Playing Dumb. Is that friend you do not know what's going on? Or will they feign ignorance to prevent shouldering additional workload? Playing stupid is a deceitful tactic that is often neglected, but if people pay attention, you will find that obvious in a lot of talented settings. If you were a community project leader at work, should you delegate the extra duty to the one member of the team who "wasn't as confident about

4

anything?" Or assign that additional responsibility to someone else? The worker who was "playing stupid" tries to get away with just doing far less but receiving the same quantity of recognition in the group as everyone else. When a community of friends is in disagreement, could one person who "doesn't realize what's going on" say the truth? Or may they be feigning ignorance, realizing full well that they were solely liable for causing the conflict? In a loving relationship, can your spouse, who "doesn't know what you're talking about," tell the truth about a problem when you interrogate them? Or could they be "acting foolish" to stop getting swept up in a lie? The "innocent party" may not have been so innocent at times, after all.

Law #11 - Pointing the Finger at Others. In the first place, a manipulator would always strive to maintain their hands clean, never take accountability, and in the second place by always attempting to point a finger at somebody else because they get off brit-free when a problem arises. Particularly when that issue might endanger their credibility and reveal them besides who they are. You could be trying to deal with a manipulator if you know someone in your relatives, mates, or even with other coworkers who always criticize everything and anyone other than themselves. Keep an eye out for anyone who's behavior pattern always involves making someone the scapegoat.

Law #12 - Telling You What You Want to Hear. When you're flattered, it's impossible not to think good and you're more willing to like the person who does all the fashionable more than the others. If one person constantly asks you all the stuff you want to learn in your life, wouldn't you be more likely to pursue them or invest more time around them? It's impossible not to think good about such people but tell you all the stuff you would like to listen to is not certainly a better friend's sign. They might be buttering you so that at a later date they can money in on a big favor that you will be "guilty" to help them with "because they were so nice to you."

Law #13 - Controlling Your Decisions. A classic setting is within a loving relationship when there is manipulation in regulating another's decision. While it is completely normal for your partner to base or start changing your decisions, is it because there is a genuine desire within you to make them happy? Or do you do it because you don't want them to risk getting angry? There is a very fine line in one relationship between what constitutes deception. If you find yourself with friends canceling schemes far too often because your partner conveys their disappointment or makes you feel bad, manipulation in the play. It's a subtle type of coercion if you keep from wearing clothing that your partner criticizes or having a haircut after your partner said "they don't like short hair" They are manipulating the choices without actually making it clear they are. It could start casually enough with a comment or two, with something so negligible like conveying how the clothes you wear don't look better on you. The kind of dress you wear should be something else especially if you find that their things have turned into nothing more than decisions that don't make you happy because they are dictated by somebody who claims to love you.

Chapter 2: Tips to Protect Yourself from Manipulation

Here are the practical tips to protect yourself from manipulation you could use to keep your mind and emotions safe every day.

- Keeping Close Connections, You Can Trust-Keeping close contact with family and friends you can trust will keep the manipulator's mind-control efforts on you to a minimum. The family and friends you can trust can give you the support you need and strengthen your self-confidence, so the manipulator has no room to plant their seeds of doubt or shake your faith.

- Speak to Your Friends and Family-Another reason the manipulator never allows you to detach from those you love and trust because you can still trust them to have your best heart interest. Those who love you (in a non-manipulative fashion) will always look to your safety. If you're ever unsure if you're subjected to manipulation (though you may have your suspicions), talk to them about what's going on and see how they react. Their immediate response-if it is shock and anger-should serve the wake-up call you need something that may not be entirely correct.

- Choosing Not to Tolerate Your Moods — Relationship manipulators sometimes sulk or resort to temperatures to get things done. If you allow them, the only one that takes an emotional toll on this kind of conduct is you. Choose not to tolerate it by walking away from the situation every time they resort to such behavior. Explain why you should not put up with this, and if they fail to change their ways, it might be time to doubt whether there is any need to hold on to this relationship for a long time.

- Ignore them-It is the best practical advice that you can find on your own. Ignore them because your time, effort, and emotions are not worth wasting on. Ignore them when they are trying to give you "advice." Ignore them as they try and tell you what to do, just go ahead and do what you wanted to do anyway. Manipulators can never be trusted, and they are always going to try to get you to do their dirty work. When you seek to hold them to account, they are going to refuse all accountability. They flip flop, go back and forth, and change their minds as often as they change clothes. Ignore them and forget everything they say; this is the only thing you can do.

- Don't try to correct them when you do, you just sink deeper into their trap. Remember, they're trying to confuse you enough so you can't see what they're up to when you're an emotional wreck and whenever you're trying to "fix" the situation, it's too easy for them to twist you around their little finger. These little traps are often set to see how you respond so they can figure out your triggers and use them to their advantage. Do not communicate, do not answer, and do not seek to correct them. It is a never-winning game.

- Don't doubt yourself-the the manipulator needs you to do just that. Why is that exactly what you shouldn't be doing? You know yourself better than anyone else might ever have, and you shouldn't have to depend on affirmation from someone to let you know you're good enough just the way you're. What separates the successful individuals from all the others is that they don't base their self-worth on someone else's opinions.

We depend on their judgment, and that's perfect if we make mistakes along the way. They are learning from it and coming back up again. Believing in yourself can be among your most potent defenses against an attack by a manipulator.

- Quit Trying So Hard to Fit in The Wrong Crowd-If you've got to work too hard to fit in with a group of people, they're not the right group for you. Manipulators are charming and popular enough to make you feel like you're part of their crowd, and they love feeling in control by making you work hard to earn their approval. They know that keeping you in this state enables them to get away with more "favor" because you will be more than willing to do what they just want to feel accepted. Don't let yourself be subjected to their manipulative ways any longer unless they can accept you for who you are; don't worry, there are plenty of other people who will. Each time you've had to work so hard to feel welcomed, that means you're working hard for the wrong people.

- Don't compromise-Undermining your own beliefs and principles is one of the many significant mistakes you might make when dealing with a manipulator. When you go against everything you believe in just to do what they want, you play right into their hands. It's all right if they make you feel bad or guilty (just another one of their tricks), let them do whatever they want. What's important is that you don't compromise your happiness, emotions, time, and energy in circles that try to accommodate them anymore. Ask yourself this: If the roles were reversed, would they be willing to do the same for you? Go back to basic rules once again, where you have the right to put your happiness and your needs first.

- Don't ask for permission-It's a hard habit to ask for permission to break. Ever since we were children, we have been taught to do that, asking our parents for permission whenever we wanted to do something. We had to ask the teachers in school for permission for the things we needed. As adults, we ask our supervisors or managers for permission before taking action. We ask permission from our partners in a relationship to get their approval before we make a move. Asking for permission can be a tough habit to break because of this. When you allow the manipulator to be in charge, you are continually seeking consent and demanding permission, rather than taking control and making your own decisions. Isn't it time to end this? This is your life, after all, and not theirs. Why are you waiting around to get their permission to tell you what to do?

- Choose Your Own Intent-You certainly don't want to do what the manipulator wants you to do. Those operating without a sense of purpose make it easier for those with a stronger will and agenda to control themselves. That is why manipulators continue to be influential today because so many people go around without a sense of purpose, leaving themselves open to being exploited. If you don't have a good sense of your own identity, you're more likely to believe what you're told and do what you're ordered to do. Because you don't have that bigger purpose of focusing on, of basing your choices on. The bigger purpose that dictates what you are ready to do and what you are not. It is easy to spot other people around you who may not even have a strong sense of purpose.

They're the ones who often flit without any real rhyme or reason throughout their lives. They are the ones who work useless jobs that either inspire or fill them with happiness, yet they do not have any real desire to change the situation. They are the ones who spend far too much time concentrating on negative gossip and other meaningless information that does not serve any real purpose. This lack of focus is what manipulators are just waiting to pounce on, so it's time to start thinking long and hard about what your goal will be if you haven't found your sense of purpose yet. Give yourself something specific to concentrate on, and you're less likely to fall victim to temptation and deceit.

- Take on New Challenges-there are new possibilities all around you; all you need to do is be bold enough to take a risk and a leap of faith. Manipulators tend to stop you from taking on new opportunities, and in the same process, they want to tie you down. They want you to live in the same loop that you are because this makes it much easier for them to retain control. That's why they are sowing seeds of self-doubt in your mind, and why they're working hard to discourage you from improving yourself or seizing new chances. Every time you grow more durable and more comfortable, you lose their grip over you, which they work hard to prevent. They're going to try too hard to keep you in your place; they're going to even resort to making you feel ashamed even to entertain the thought of taking on new opportunities to improve yourself. Don't let them stop you, and don't let go of self-doubt. Even successful people made many mistakes along the way to get to where they are right now; all they did was have the courage to take the leap and make a change for the better.

- Stop Being a Punching Bag-Manipulators will only continue to treat you as a punching bag if you allow them to do so. Respect yourself enough to stand up and say you're not worthy of this type of treatment. Because, you are not. Stop being a punching bag, start taking responsibility for your decisions, and remember that there's no reason to feel guilty about standing up to someone who doesn't treat you fairly.

Manipulators will always seek to do whatever they can to undermine your faith and weaken you enough to take control of you. They will claim to be concerned about you, or that they just have the best interest in mind. They will convince you they want to "help," when the truth is, they will be the only person they want to help, and if they have to step on their toes to do so, they will. They can be hard to get rid of once you bring them into your life, but your know-how can be done now. The final key is never to stop working to build your self-confidence, the healthier you are, the less control they have over you.

Chapter 3: Reasons of Manipulation and How to Overcome It

The only time when manipulation is considered successful is the time when you allow it to control your emotions and thoughts. Thus, you must start to distinguish what is going on in you that allows you to be easily manipulated by other people. The three most basic reasons we let ourselves to be manipulated are as follows:

• Fear

This emotion comes in numerous structures. As human beings, we tend to fear losing a relationship; we may fear the disapprobation of other people; we dread to make somebody discontent with our actions. We additionally dread the dangers and outcomes of the manipulator's actions. Imagine a scenario in which they prevail at doing what they threaten.

• Guilt

Today, we are clouded by the idea and responsibility that we should dependably prioritize other people's needs and wants rather than our own. At times when people would talk about the right to fulfill their own needs and wants, manipulators frequently abuse us and endeavor to allow us to feel like we are accomplishing something immoral if we do not generally put their needs and wants in front of our own. Those individuals who are skilled at these manipulative tactics would tend to define love as the act of fulfilling their needs and wants as part of your obligation. Hence, if we have an opinion that goes against their beliefs, we are manipulated into thinking that we are heartless; at this point, they would make us feel very regretful of our existence and would use guilt to manipulate us.

- Being too nice

We appreciate being a provider, fulfilling individuals, and dealing with the needs of other people. We discover fulfillment. Moreover, our confidence would regularly originate from doing what we can for other people. In any case, at times when there is a lack of an unmistakable feeling of these and fair limitations, skilled manipulators can detect this in people who are easy targets of this phenomenon, and will use certain tactics to further their selfish gains.

What You Need To Do To Overcome Manipulation

We have come to a point where we are here to talk about the basic skills to overcome manipulation. Moreover, manipulation would only work if you allow them to control you. Much like hypnosis, any hypnosis is self-hypnosis. We are trying to state here that knowledge that you are being manipulated defeats its entire purpose.

- Establish a clear sense of self

There is a need to know your identity, your needs and wants, what your emotions are, and what you are fond of and not fond of. You must learn to accept these and not become apologetic, as these are the things that make you. At times, we dread that we are viewed by others as egotistical and called out for being selfish in the event of speaking up. Nevertheless, knowing your identity or what you need in life is not at all an act of selfishness. Self-centeredness demands that you always get what you want or that other has always put your needs and wants first. Similarly, when another person calls you out for not following their orders or fulfilling their needs and wants, they are the ones being selfish, not you.

- Say "no" despite the other person's disapproval

The ability to say "no" despite somebody's objection is a solid demonstration. Individuals who can do this are present in reality. Because in reality, there is no way that we can accommodate all of their needs and wants. When this happens, they will become baffled, even disappointed. However, keep in mind that what they are feeling is part of human nature. Most of these individuals would then forgive and forget. Sound individuals realize that getting what you want all the time is not possible, even when the desires are genuine. In any case, when we cannot endure another person's mistake or objection, it ends up hard stating "no." It winds up more diligently for us to state it or have limits. Manipulators exploit this shortcoming and use dissatisfaction and objection in extraordinary structures to get us to do what they need.

- Tolerate the other person's negative affect

We can demonstrate compassion for people's pity, hurt, or even annoyance when accommodating them without needing to back down and reverse our decision. Keep in mind, a solid relationship is described by common minding, shared genuineness, and shared regard. If you are involved with somebody who uses manipulation and unhealthy control consistently, begin to see little propensities that may not be clear to you at first. As you are more grounded, you are better ready to endure how the other individual's negative impact on you is only bringing you down. Thus, this turns into a positive development that liberates you from their manipulative grasps. This will engender a complexity of sorts with the people in your life. The manipulator may start to withdraw and consider your time, emotions, wants, and needs, or they will proceed onward to someone else who is an easy target of manipulation practices.

Chapter 4: Character Traits of a Manipulator

Is language the primary tool of deviously manipulative people? How can words have such a powerful effect on us?

How a manipulative person's mind works, is most likely only something a manipulative person could comprehend. The rest of us think about in confusion, wondering why or how someone could behave this way. Though, in some small way, we can all be a little manipulative at times. For example, most people will be willing to bend the truth, or omit information, on the odd occasion. For much the same reasons, such as trying to get others to do something for them or even to get permission for something. Trying to convince someone of your argument or get them to come around to your way of thinking, is a natural and evolutionary process. Pinker and Bloom (1990) claimed that we evolved to use language because it helped us adapt to our environments. Surviving hostile elements is easier if we can persuade others to help us persevere.

The use of language to manipulate others to help us is the evolutionary adaptation, appears to be a natural process. Why then, do some individuals manipulate others for more pervasive means? Not for survival or evolutionary means, but purely for their own selfish needs. If they cannot achieve this control, they feel helpless and lack any agency in their lives. Why? Are they evil, are they unkind, are they born that way? Some might say it is a personality disorder that is bordering on a narcissistic level.

We will all try to persuade someone at some point in our lives, but we are not all narcissists. Whatever the reason for our attempts at persuasion, we usually want to remain on good terms with the person we are trying to manipulate. Not so for those who manipulate to control.

Kier Harding, a lead Mental Health practitioner, wrote a relevant article in The Diagnosis of Exclusion. He argued that those diagnosed with a personality disorder are people who are not very good at manipulating. Their attempts tend to be forceful and over exaggerated. Whereas a skillful manipulator will aim to persuade someone less overtly. It is because they are not very good at it, that makes them unlikable characters with poor interpersonal skills. Usually also with a low self-esteem because of their background in life. This could be an argument indicating that controlling manipulators are from dysfunctional backgrounds.

How Then Can We Recognize Such A Deviant Person?

Common Traits

Use of Language

We have shown how powerful language can be, as a prime tool of persuasion. There is more to the manipulative controller though than mere words. They will use tactics that mislead and unbalance their target's inner thoughts. We now understand that through language, they will:

- Use mistruths to mislead and confuse their target's normal thinking pattern.
- Force their target to decide speed, so they don't have time to analyze and think.
- Overwhelmingly talk to their target, making them feel small.
- Criticize their target's judgment so they begin to lose their self-esteem.

- Raise the tone of their voice and not be afraid to use aggressive body language.
- Ignore their target's needs, they are only interested in getting what they want and at any cost.

Invasion of Personal Space

Most of us set boundaries around ourselves without realizing we are doing so. It is a kind of unspoken rule to protect our private space, such as not sitting so close that you are touching another person, especially a stranger. A manipulative character cares nothing about overstepping such boundaries. Whether this is because they do not understand, or they do not care is unclear. Initially, they are unlikely to invade their target's personal space. They will seek to build up a good rapport first. This shows that they understand boundaries because once they gain the confidence of their target, they will then ignore them.

Fodder For Thought

Manipulators tend to be very ego-centric, with limited social skills. Their only concern is for themselves. Everything they do in life will be about how it affects them, not how their actions affect others. Does this mean that they have a psychopathic disorder?

Take empathy for instance. Controlling manipulators are unlikely ever to show empathy. Empathy is a natural human emotion that aids in our survival techniques. A study by Meffert et al. indicates that those with a psychopathic disorder can control empathetic emotions. They lack sympathy of any kind because another weakness is simply another tool for them. When they detect any weakness in their target's resolve or personality, they will exploit it. The consequences to their victim are of little importance. The targets weakness's feed the manipulator's strength, making them bolder and often crueler in their actions.

Creating Rivalry

Another tactic of the controlling manipulator is backstabbing. They may tell you how great a person you are to your face, making themselves look good. Behind your back, they are busy spreading malicious gossip and untruths about you. This is a classic trait of a controlling manipulator as it creates a rivalry between people. Then, they can pick sides that will make them look favorable, particularly to their target. It can act as the first stage to getting close to their target. Once bonded, they can build up trust, making it easier to manipulate the target in the future. If you recognize a backstabber, keep them at a distance. Their plan is selfish so it is better not let them into your personal life. There is no point treating them as they treat you, in revenge. It will turn out to be exhausting playing them at their own game. If they know that you are on to them, they may attempt to lure you back with praise, remember that it is false.

Domineering Personality

It is unlikely that a manipulative person will outwardly show any form of weakness. An important part of their facade is to show conviction about their views. They seek to impress, believing they are right about everything. Almost to the point that if they realize they are wrong, they will still argue that they are right. On a one-to-one level, that invariably means that your position is always wrong. As they will chip away at your beliefs, they seek to undermine your sense of self-esteem. Once they have achieved this, then there is no holding them back. They seek to domineer others, often speaking with a condescending tone to belittle their victims. Using ridicule is yet another tool against their target, merely because it will make themselves look better. If you ridicule them back, they will seek to turn the tables, accusing you of being oversensitive to their "joke." The kind of joke that only the teller sees the funny side.

Passive Aggressive Behavior

A common trait of many hard-core manipulators is passive aggressive behavior. Because they prefer to be popular, they do not wish to be seen as doing anything wrong. Not that a manipulator would ever admit to doing anything wrong. They are experts with facial expressions that are meant to dominate and intimidate. This may include; knitting eyebrows, grinding teeth and rolling eyes. It may also include noises such as tutting and grunting sounds. It is a very common behavior for such a character, as little anyone else has to say that they will agree upon. For most manipulators, it is their life's ambition to show people up by proving them wrong.

This can range from the confrontational look, where they seek to stare their target down. Or, It could be in response to their disagreement on something their target said. They may smirk and shake their head, turn their back, anything to show their strong disapproval. It is all a ploy to make themselves look superior and put others down.

Moody Blues

What of emotional stability of the manipulator? Is it that which makes them behave the way they do? Do they even know what happiness is? The answer to that is a most definite yes, at least to the latter.

Happiness is a tool used initially to help them manipulate, a happy target is more likely to comply. In itself, this makes the manipulator happy, or at least in a sense of what they consider happiness. But their joyfulness is a perverted model of what most others consider happiness to be. Their happiness is often built on the foundations of another's misery. A misery that they have caused with their cruel manipulations. Equally though, a manipulator is prone to mood swings. Most likely to happen when things are not going to plan. One minute they are euphoric at their latest conquest. Then next they could be completely deflated at their failure to succeed. One thing is certain for those who live with or become a target of this type of domineering character, they will be unhappy all the time.

Intimidation

One aspect of manipulation, often used as a last resort, is intimidation and bullying. When everything else has failed, they begin to use threats to get their way. Some though may use intimidation from the onset. It may in a source of authority. For example, let's take the role of a manipulative boss. You have requested a day off. They don't want to allow you your request but have no choice, it is your right. This type of person would want their pound of flesh first. They will set goals for you to reach so it will delay or cancel your request, such as moving project deadlines forward. This way they have their little victory over you.

Alternatively, such a manipulator may use the tactic of the silent treatment. Ignoring someone to the point that it becomes obvious you have displeased them. They seek to make you feel the guilty party.

Other more direct intimidating actions may include stance. Using their height or build to tower over you, or standing uncomfortably close.

Be careful as they will seek revenge for wrongdoings they perceive done to them. Nothing will go unnoticed under their watchful eye. Everyone is a potential target. But, the weak are more likely to walk into their traps, because they are the ones who are easier to dominate. The vulnerable will have little resistance and are easier to bully and coerce. Many of these traits seem more fitting to men, but women can be cruelly manipulative too.

This is a person who will never back down in an argument. Never admit they are wrong. Never apologize for anything. A manipulator will never show respect but will expect everyone else to show them respect.

They love nothing more than to embarrass others. Playing the dumb one is common practice, just to force another person to explain themselves further. At every opportunity, the manipulator will jump in with some sarcastic remark, "hurry up, we're all waiting for your intellectual explanation," or "why has no one else ever heard of this?" Their sole aim is to make the other person look a fool, but without seeming to be the one who made it happen. Oh no, the victim did that to themselves because they are stupid.

Chapter 5: Behavioral Traits of Favorite Victims of Manipulators

Certain characteristics and behavioral traits make people more vulnerable to manipulation, and people with dark psychology traits know this full well. They tend to seek out victims who have those specific behavioral traits because they are essentially easy targets. Let's discuss 6 of the traits of the favorite victims of manipulators.

Emotional Insecurity and Fragility

Manipulators like to target victims who are emotionally insecure or emotionally fragile. Unfortunately for these victims, such traits are very easy to identify even in total strangers, so it's easy for experienced manipulators to find them.

Emotionally insecure people tend to be very defensive when they are attacked or under pressure, making them easy to spot in social situations. Even after just a few interactions, a manipulator can gauge how insecure a person is with a certain degree of accuracy. They'll try to provoke their potential targets subtly, and then wait to see how they react. If they are overly defensive, manipulators will take it as a sign of insecurity, and they will intensify their manipulative attacks.

Manipulators can also tell if a target is emotionally insecure if he/she redirects accusations or negative comments. They will find a way to put you on the spot, and if you try to throw it back at them or make excuses instead of confronting the situation head-on, the manipulator could conclude that you are insecure and therefore an easy target.

People who have social anxiety also tend to have emotional insecurity, and manipulators are aware of it. In social gatherings, they can easily spot individuals who have social anxiety, then target them for manipulation. "Pickup artists" can identify the girls who seem uneasy in social situations by conducting themselves. Social anxiety is difficult to conceal, especially to manipulators who are experienced at preying on emotional vulnerability.

Emotional fragility is different from emotional insecurity. Emotionally insecure people tend to show it all the time, while emotionally fragile people appear to be normal, but they break down emotionally at the slightest provocation. Manipulators like targeting emotionally fragile people because it's very easy to elicit a reaction from them. Once a manipulator finds out that you are emotionally fragile, he will jump at the change to manipulate you because he knows it would be fairly easy.

Sensitive People

Highly sensitive people are those individuals who process information at a deeper level and are more aware of the subtleties in social dynamics. They have lots of positive attributes because they tend to be very considerate of others, and they watch their step to avoid causing people any harm, whether directly or indirectly. Such people tend to dislike any form of violence or cruelty, and they are easily upset by news reports about disastrous occurrences, or even depictions of gory scenes in movies.

Sensitive people also tend to get emotionally exhausted from taking in other people's feelings. When they walk into a room, they have the immediate ability to detect other people's moods, because they are naturally skilled at identifying and interpreting other people's body language cues, facial expressions, and tonal variations.

Manipulators like to target sensitive people because they are easy to manipulate. If you are sensitive to certain things, manipulators can use them against you. They will feign certain emotions to draw sensitive people in so that they can exploit them.

Sensitive people also tend to scare easily. They have a heightened "startle reflex," which means that they are more likely to show clear signs of fear or nervousness in potentially threatening situations. For example, sensitive people are more likely to jump up when someone sneaks up on them, even before determining whether they are in any real danger. If you are a sensitive person, this trait can be very difficult to hide, and malicious people will see it from a mile away.

Manipulators can also identify sensitive people by listening to how they talk. Sensitive people tend to be very proper; they never use vulgar language, and they tend to be very politically correct because they are trying to avoid offending anyone. They also tend to be polite, and they say please and thank you more often than others. Manipulators go after such people because they know that they are too polite to dismiss them right away; sensitive people will indulge anyone because they don't want to be rude. That gives maliciously people a way in.

Emphatic People

Emphatic people are generally similar to highly sensitive people, except that they are more attuned to others' feelings and the energy of the world around them. They tend to internalize other people's suffering to the point that it becomes their own. In fact, for some of them, it can be difficult to distinguish someone's discomfort from their own. Emphatic people make the best partners because they feel everything you feel. However, this makes them particularly easy to manipulate, so malicious people like to target them.

Malicious people can feign certain emotions, and convey those emotions to emphatic people, who will feel them as real. That opens them up for exploitation. Emphatic people are the favorite targets of psychopathic conmen because they feel so deeply for others. A conman can make up stories about financial difficulties and swindle lots of money from emphatic people.

The problem with being emphatic is that because you have such strong emotions, you easily dismiss your doubts about people because you would much rather offer help to a person who turns out to be a lair than deny help to a person who turns out to be telling the truth.

Malicious people like to get into relationships with emphatic people because they are easy to take advantage of. Emphatic people try to avoid getting into intimate relationships in the first place because they know that it's easy for them to get engulfed in such relationships and to lose their identities in the process. However, manipulators will doggedly pursue them because they know that they can guilt the emphatic person into doing anything they want once they get it.

Fear of Loneliness

Many people are afraid of being alone, but this fear is heightened in a small percentage of the population. This kind of fear can be truly paralyzing for those who experience it, and it can open them up to exploitation by malicious people. For example, many people stay in dysfunctional relationships because they are afraid, they will never find someone else to love them if they break up with an abusive partner. Manipulators can identify this fear in a victim, and they'll often do everything they can to fuel it further to make sure that the person is crippled by it. People who are afraid of being alone can tolerate or even rationalize any kind of abuse.

The fear of being alone can be easy to spot in a potential victim. People with this kind of fear tend to exude some desperation level at the beginning of relationships, and they can sometimes come across as clingy. While ordinary people may think of being clingy as a red flag, manipulative people will see it as an opportunity to exploit somebody. If you are attached to them, they'll use manipulative techniques to become even more dependent on them. They can withhold love and affection (e.g., by using the silent treatment) to make the victim fear that he/she is about to get dumped so that they act out of desperation and cede more control to the manipulator.

The fear of being alone is, for the most part, a social construct, and it disproportionately affects women more than men. For generations, our society has taught women that their goal in life is to get married and have children. Even the more progressive women who reject this social construct are still plagued by social pressures to adhere to those old standards. That being said, the fact is that men also tend to be afraid of being alone.

People with abandonment issues stemming from childhood tend to experience the fear of loneliness to a higher degree. Some may not necessarily fear loneliness in general, but they are afraid of being separated from important people. For example, many people end up staying in abusive or dysfunctional relationships because they are afraid of being separated from their children.

Fear of Disappointing Others

We all feel a certain sense of obligation towards the people in our lives, but some are extremely afraid of disappointing others. This kind of fear is similar to the fear of embarrassment and the fear of rejection because it means that the person puts a lot of stock into how others perceive them. The fear of disappointing others can occur naturally. It can be useful in some situations; parents who are afraid of disappointing their families will work harder to provide for them, and children who are afraid of disappointing their parents will study harder at school. In this case, the fear is constructive. However, it becomes unhealthy when directed at the wrong people, or when it forces you to compromise your comfort and happiness.

When manipulators find out that you have a fear of disappointing others, they'll try to put you in a position where you feel like you owe them something. They'll do certain favors for you, and then they'll manipulate you into believing that you have a sense of obligation towards them. They will then guilt you into complying with any request whenever they want something from you.

Personality Dependent Disorders and Emotional Dependency

Dependent personality disorder refers to a real disorder characterized by a person having an excessive and even pervasive need to be taken care of. This need often leads the person to be submissive towards the people in their lives and be clingy and afraid of separation. People with this disorder act in ways that are meant to elicit caregiving. They tend to practice what's called "learned helplessness." This is where they act out of a conviction that they cannot do certain things for themselves, and they need the help of others.

31

Manipulators like to target people with dependent personality disorders because they are very easy to control and dominate. These people willingly cede control over their lives to others, so when manipulators come knocking, they don't face much resistance. Manipulators start by giving them a false sense of security, but once they have won their trust, they switch gears and start imposing their will on them.

Emotional dependency is somewhat similar to dependent personality disorder, but it doesn't rise to clinical significance. It stems from having low self-esteem, and it's often a result of childhood abandonment issues. People with an emotional dependency will play the submissive role in relationships for fear of losing their partners. They tend to be very agreeable because they want to please the people in their lives. Such people are easy to manipulate, and malicious people can easily dominate them.

Chapter 6:   Manipulators   Are Everywhere

It is worth noting that manipulative people don't always come out of nowhere. Often, we find individuals with this behavior in the workplace, at school, and in the family. The characteristics presented above are shaped according to the mode of conviviality. Here's how to deal with manipulative people in these environments:

At Work

In a professional environment, the manipulator is the employee always ready to help. But remember, it's a compulsive help. He stays at the heels of colleagues, reinforcing at all times how much he loves helping colleagues who have difficulties in their tasks. The manipulator on the desktop can stay up later, and even take a break in the office, all for the "pleasure of helping others". The targets of "goodwill" are charmed with such dedication.

The manipulator is seen as the company's legal person, employee and fellow in charge in most of the work. However, this establishes a relationship of dependence. Whoever is the target of "goodwill" is being placed in a web. The one who receives the "help" loses his autonomy since he cannot act without asking for the manipulator's opinion. Consequently, he loses confidence and does everything not to lose this "friendship". When the victim begins to perceive himself as such and tries to escape, the manipulator reverses the roles and convinces his prey that he is bad. The prey, in turn, accepts such a condition and follows the will of his tormentor.

- How to get rid of the manipulator at work?

Be firm and kindly dispense unsolicited favors. When the manipulator takes the day off to flatter you, return the compliments, but make it clear that you are just doing your duty, and anyone else would do the same. The manipulator will be amazed at your steadiness.

In School

At school, the manipulator is the perfect colleague. The manipulator targets unpopular students who are constantly ridiculed.

The manipulator praises the high notes, you are sure that the "new friend" is the best student. When his grades are low, he places the teacher's blame because the teacher certainly did it to harm him. He does not hesitate to defend injustice. There is no bad time that prevents you from helping with the activities and the manipulator makes a point of doing the work with you. The target of such unknowing friendship reveals what time he leaves home, what time it takes to drive there, reveals possible enmities with other students, tells of his fears and anguish. The manipulator reveals nothing about his life.

When the victim begins to realize that something is strange and tries to disengage, the manipulator feels extremely offended. He places the "friend" as an unjust person, unable to recognize true friendship. The manipulator depreciates the "friend", listing his defects, and claims that he will return to being a solitary person and be ridiculed if the friendship ends. The prey, who already had low self-esteem, is even more vulnerable. Thus, the victim believes the manipulator, apologizes, and no longer measures their efforts to do all the manipulator's will, so afraid of losing the "friendship".

- How to get rid of the manipulator in school?

If you feel that you are being cheated again, move away slowly. Speak only as necessary and ask other people's opinions on how to deal with the situation.

In The Family

In the family, the manipulator sticks close to that shy relative and is considered good by everyone. It may be that cousin who always compliments, even when the victim has done something that isn't so great. The manipulator justifies his "object of affection" blockades and believes that his target is wronged. He insists on telling us how much he loves us and is happy to be with such special people.

The manipulator is always ready to go to the mall, help with school activities, go to the doctor's office and do some repairs. However, when the target begins to be bothered by the excessive clinginess and flattery, the manipulator turns the tables and lowers his victim. The manipulator underscores his lack of social skills and how he is seen as lonely, poor, and unable to have friends. The sentences that the victim says will continue to be seen as unimportant. The already emotionally unstable target agrees with everything, apologizes, and resumes "friendship", doing everything according to his tormentor's will, afraid of not being able to count on such a valuable person.

- How to get rid of the manipulator in the family?

Family ties make things harder. But we must put an end to this vicious circle. Ask the opinion of people outside the family spectrum. Even if it is not possible to cut the manipulator out of the conversation, talk only when necessary.

Differences Between Male And Female Manipulators

The behavior between men and women is different in several respects. In the question of manipulation, there are also singularities.

Men

Male manipulators have the following characteristics:

Shy: The manipulator observes the behavior of everyone around him. He transmits fragility and submission to convince himself that he is a needy person;

Handsome: Manipulators are always friendly, extroverted and know how to live life. They show extremely worried and attentive with their "friends", but they make a point of showing who is in charge. The victims do not feel the courage to disagree with such a nice man. But when he goes to a boring event, he does not bother to disguise his boredom;

Altruist: He gives many gifts, does numerous favors, always intending to receive something in return. When it is not "retributed" it gives people a sense of guilt;

Seductive: Vain and attractive. He looks into others' eyes, asks embarrassing questions and loves to make a mystery of himself;

Worship: Has excessive admiration for diplomas, pompous professional curricula, and social projection. He subtly shows contempt for those who do not have the same knowledge. He loves to embarrass people, monopolizes conversations, and gets annoyed when someone interrupts his speech.

Women

Manipulative women behave in the following ways:

In front of everyone, they are true porcelain dolls. But when the target moves away, she's stupid with people. When the victim returns she will be candid with him/her;

Use beauty as a weapon to get what she wants. It seems absurd to someone not to praise it.

She uses a sensual tone of voice and promises a thousand wonders to those who satisfy her requests; she wants the target to guess her wishes and surprise her with trips, restaurants, and luxury gifts. She becomes angry if her requests are not answered.

Her emotions can be radical. When you are right, she wants to prove that it's better that you are wrong. When she is wrong, she does not admit it and insists until someone believes in her.

They cry too much. If the victim wants to go out with other people, she cries because she was "betrayed." If she is asked how the car got scratched, she cries because she was accused of being a bad driver. She is "fragile" to the point of not carrying a suitcase or not being able to open the car door.

Manipulative people enter our lives because they see that we are going through a moment of vulnerability. We feed these people by providing intimate information. But if we allow them to enter our lives, it is up to us to remove them from the scene. The task is difficult, but these tips can be useful:

Do not feel guilty for not satisfying the wishes of the manipulator. Often they are irrational and seem like things a child who wants attention at any cost may request. Ask probing questions, question what will change if you attend to the manipulator's wishes. Ask yourself how your feelings were before and how they are now. Learn not to speak to those who do not do you good; this means you must avoid saying yes to the manipulator.

If none of this works out, move away. If it is not possible to physically get the person out of your life, move away emotionally and speak only about the basics. Remember that manipulative people are "toxic people", non-evolved beings who want to suck energy and steal others' autonomy. No one deserves to live in the shadow of others, no one deserves to live having to consult someone at every step. Emotional independence is the key to a happy existence.

Chapter 7: Understanding the Dark Triad and What It Means

Now, we need to take a look at the dark triad. This is a very important concept because it will help tie together some of the other aspects that we have in Dark Psychology. The name "dark triad" may sound like something that comes from a horror movie, but it is a legitimate psychological concept that is well recognized.

The dark triad is nothing more than an identification system for the three most destructive and harmful psychological personality traits a person can have. This will take some time to detail each of the traits, including narcissism, psychopathy, and Machiavellianism. Let's take a look at each part and see what it means when it comes to dark psychology.

What Is Machiavellianism?

The first aspect of the Dark Triad that we will discuss is known as Machiavellianism. This aspect gets its name from the political philosopher known as Machiavelli. In his classical work, "The Prince," the ideas, principles, and tactics used by those who seek to influence others are outlined. But how exactly does a Machiavellian person come across?

The hallmarks of this trait include a willingness to focus on your self-interest all the time, an understanding of the importance of your image, the perception of appearance, and even the ruthless exercise of power and cruelty rather than using mercy or compassion.

To keep it simple, people who have this trait always have a strategy when approaching life. The consequences and any ramifications about any action will be thought out and then assessed in terms of how they will impact the one who is carrying them out. The Machiavellian approach to the world is summed up with a simple question: "How will this action benefit me, and how will my public perception be impacted as a result?"

Machiavellian people will be masters of doing what is going to personally serve them well, while still being able to maintain the good public image that they want. This allows the manipulator to do what they want, while getting people around them to like them still.

What Is Psychopathy?

The next aspect that we will discuss is psychopathy. This will refer to a psychological condition that involves a superficial charm, impulsivity, and a lack of commonly held human emotions, such as remorse and empathy. Someone who exhibits enough of these traits can be known as a psychopath. These individuals are seen as some of the most dangerous people because they can hide their true intentions while still causing a lot of trouble.

People often associate the word "psychopath" with an image of madness and wields a machete. The reality is different, and this can make it more deadly. A true psychopath is more likely to be that charming and handsome stranger who can win over their victim before they ruin their lives.

Interestingly, some of the top people in business score high on psychopathy personality tests. But as time goes on, it is becoming more common to see psychopathy as more of a problem to the victim and society rather than an issue in the psychopath's own life. Psychopaths can get to the top of anything they choose because they don't have to worry about some of the compassionate indecision that other humans will experience.

What Is Narcissism?

The third aspect of the Dark Triad that we need to explore is narcissism. This is often thought of like the idea that a person loves themselves too much. This is close but quite the right definition for someone who is a narcissist. You can have self-love without being considered a narcissist.

Someone who is considered a narcissist is likely to have a range of traits that are there. They will have an overly inflated self-worth, such as seeing that their lives are extra special and one of the most important lives in history. If this has been inflated enough, they may see that they are the most important in the world.

In the mind of a narcissist, they are not only special, but they are superior to everyone else. They consider themselves to be a better species of person, higher than what normal people would be. And because a narcissist believes this way, their behaviors are going to change. The behavior that you see in a narcissist is going to reflect the self-worth that the person has.

Some of the outward signs or manifestations of this aspect would include the person's inability to accept any dissent or criticism of any kind. Even if they feel that someone is trying to criticize them, they will have a hard time dealing with this. This kind of person also feels the need to have others agree with them all the time, and they like to be flattered. If you are around someone who seems always to need constant praise, recognition, and approval, and if they seem to organize their lives to give them constant access to those who will fill this need, then it is likely that you are dealing with someone who is a narcissist.

These three aspects are going to come together to form the Dark Triad. When one person has all of these three traits in them, it can be a hard task to stay away and not get pulled into whatever plan they have. Being on the lookout for these can make a big difference in how much control you have in your personal life.

Chapter 8: Mind Games

When a person plays "mind games" on us, it is attributed to being innocent. Many people have come across this at some point in their life. Take an example when someone is planning a surprise party and doesn't want the other person to know and he does this by playing mind tricks not to give away what the surprise is. This is merely considered innocent and silly. Dark psychology mind games are not in any way innocent. Mind games in dark psychology are attributed to the hypnotist toying with his victim's will power and sanity. This differs from other dark psychological manipulation in the sense that the manipulator is playing with his victim for his pleasure and enjoyment and is not invested in what the outcome will be. His interest in the victim would be to test the victim so to speak. Mind games are used by a hypnotist when other forms of suggestions to the victim are not effective and may decide to use mind games which are rather less obvious to the audience. The manipulator may decide to use mind games to his pleasure and amusement. Mind games are very effective in reducing the assuredness and psychological strength of the victim. The victim is eluded into thinking that he still has control. Manipulators can satisfy their twisted amusement when playing mind games. Such dark psychological manipulators do not see their victims as equal human beings. Instead, they choose to see the victim as a 'toy' and, therefore, watch with amusement when victims do what they tell them to. Sometimes, a dark manipulator will have known mind games all his life and knows no other forms of dark psychology manipulation. These manipulators can be dangerous because they know not of any other option and therefore no need to change and be more humane. Let us dive into the specific types of mind games used by dark manipulators.

Ultimatum

An ultimatum can be defined as a final proposition or condition. One, therefore, is presented with a severe choice. They are viewed more as demands other than a request. An example is, "Be more outgoing...or I will see other people". Certain factors will decide whether an ultimatum will be considered as a mind game. The three factors are one, the type of person giving the ultimatum, second the intention for giving the ultimatum and lastly the nature of the ultimatum.

Persons who give ultimatums and genuinely care about the persons and have a valid reason for doing so, and then it will fall under the non-dark manipulation. These persons will generally include spouses, parents, siblings or close relatives. However, if they fall into any of the categories mentioned, it does not necessarily rid them of dark intentions from the ultimatum.

What was the intention of the person giving the ultimatum? People with good intentions are often driven by the desire to help or assist in bettering a person's life. A person gives an ultimatum to stop smoking or drinking too much, then this seen as good intentions. Being able to tell the intention of an ultimatum is difficult, so looking at the nature of the ultimatum itself is the surest way to tell whether it is dark.

Dark manipulative ultimatums will involve the person doing something that goes against what they stand for and goes against their self-interest. The victim ends up comprising their moral standards in the process. Manipulators test their victims to see how far they go in compromising what they believe in. As we have seen, non-dark ultimatums are usually to benefit another person and the does not have to go against what they know is wrong.

What is a dark psychological ultimatum? The person giving the ultimatum will be a friend, a boss or a person who the victim is in a toxic relationship with. It could also the form of a spouse, a parent or a sibling. The manipulator will often give ultimatums that go against the victim's moral conviction or possibly be dangerous to the victim. Here, the dark manipulator will notice a disinclination towards something and take advantage of this to make their victim do their bidding.

An example will be a girl who is not comfortable in wearing costumes or revealing clothes. Some of the ultimatums will be, "It's an only costume party, it is either you wear one or you are not invited". Some ultimatums lead to harm to others such as assault and even murder. At very extreme cases, the victim ends up taking his own life in completing a suicide pact in which the manipulator does not honor his end.

The External Break Up

Everybody likes to be in a relationship where there is that sense of security and knowing that your partner is content. A manipulator will know this but will use these for their dark intentions. A manipulator will ensure that their partner will be powerless by instigating feelings of instability, and negativity. This technique of 'The External Break up' is often deployed in a romantic relationship. It manifests itself when a partner continuously to scares the other that he or she will leave them. This is aimed at creating feelings of anxiety and instability within the relationship. This mind game takes the form of promised breakups, implied breakups and actual breakups that do not happen.

Implied breakups are those that are not expressly stating the words 'break up'. Instead, the manipulator throws hints there and then to create some doubt in the partner's mind. They can do this by making statements that exclude their partner from plans together. Promised breakups happen where the dark manipulator scares their partner instead of breaking up with them somewhere soon. Words like, "Don't worry I won't have to deal with this anymore because I'll be leaving soon" show the intention of a breakup in the future. Promise breakups fall in between the implied breakups and the actual breakups. Where the dark manipulator mentions the idea of cutting ties with their partner, either by divorcing, separating or breaking up, but does not follow through then it calls under the promised breakup.

The actual break is the most severe compared to the implied and promised breakups. It happens when the manipulator decides to leave their victim without actually leaving in the end. They may pack up their clothes and belongings in the attempt to leave but once they see the sadness all over their victim's face, they decide otherwise.

After understanding the tactic of the "external break up" we ask ourselves what therefore is the end game for manipulator when they use this tactic? The manipulator aims to have the upper hand in the relationship by creating feelings of uncertainty and lack of security from the victim's life and therefore reducing their power in the hands of the manipulator. By repeatedly simulating a breakup with the victim, the manipulator tries to test the waters of how far one will go in putting up with being treated like a toy. In the end, when the manipulator gives in to the victims' begging for the relationship to continue, they make themselves look like the generous ones. This works so well for the manipulator because his or her victim is not thinking rationally to figure out why they relationship should end. They are therefore willing to continue with the relationship. Many people do not understand this concept of dark psychology and why a person would want to continue to be in a relationship with a dark manipulator in the first place. The impact of this on the victim includes the likelihood of developing serious trust issues where they will have a hard time trusting another person. This could take a toll on the victim's professional relationships and family relationships as well. After a long period of constant threats, the victims become almost like a slave to the manipulator. The manipulator eventually grows tired and moves on to their next prey.

Hard To Get

And just like ultimatums, the hard to get tactic can easily pass off as being normal. Hard to get can be dark as it can be also harmless and normal. Hard to get when it is harmless it occurs when a person will want to make them seem trying to be with them is not as easy. They will do this by making themselves less available by not making to every date and leaving the phone to ring a couple of time before finally picking up. The 'hard to get' dark psychology is much riskier. The manipulator will use this tactic during the relationship rather than at the beginning of the relationship. Unlike the innocent hard to get where the intention is to be in a happy relationship eventually, dark psychology hard is far from taking into account the victim's wellbeing. When used at the beginning of the relationship it is innocent because no expectations are infringed. No one is dependent or reliant on either of the person, so no harm comes from playing hard to get. Further along in a relationship when things are going on well, suddenly, a person is unreliable and often tries to make themselves busy. This kind of behaviour is not normal because relationships are about making and spending time with each other as this will firm up the relationship. A manipulator will be very cunning and start pulling away when their partner us already reliant on them. The victim will therefore put an extra effort to reconnect with their partner. In the end, the manipulator has the upper hand and will use this power to his or her purpose while the victim is left in deep confusion and instability.

Chapter 9:   Mind Control Technique

Having control over everyday situations is something all human beings wish for. The ability to command what will happen is the dream of most people. Although it is impossible to accomplish 100% of the time, some techniques allow you to achieve the desired results more often. If you did not know, it is possible to influence someone's actions with simple behaviors and signals sent directly to the person you would like to impact. You can apply the following tips in meetings with your boss, at a job interview, or even with that platonic passion!

1. Honest Smile

You should know that a smile is one of the most important and significant aspects of body language, yet do you know how to give a perfect smile? Some smiles are visibly forceful and hostile, so you should seek to convey truth. But how can we maximize this action? Simply, you should keep your normal countenance and, after only a few seconds, greet the person and give him a sincere smile. Whoever smiles the most can gain greater emotional control of the other person, who will feel more comfortable with his presence.

2. Look

When you are in a group of friends and the person of your interest is there, do not hesitate to direct your attention to him/her. The tendency is to pay attention to what is being deliberated at the wheel of the conversation, but what will attract your interest's attention is the look. When you focus your eyes on the other person, you will automatically catch their attention eventually. If you know how to gauge your looks, it will soon be within your power to get their attention. If you're at a job interview or speaking to the boss, keep your eye on the eyes of the person you're talking to because this increases the chances of that person feeling greater empathy and confidence in you!

3. Be Insistent

You will be impressed by how you can persuade your friends. We already heard the famous phrase that says "A lie repeated a thousand times becomes true", right? But although we are not dealing with lies, you can apply this phrase in the present technique. If you want someone to believe and give credence to what you say, just insist on their perspective. For example, imagine that you want to sell some product and need to show that it is worth buying it. To persuade your buyer, it is no use to be insistent by repeating the same arguments because you will become inconvenient. Instead, try to increase the list of good points to gain credibility, and you will be successful.

4. Justifications

You may not trust it, but you increase your ability to convince the other person to do the desired favor when you justify your requests. Researchers conducted a test in which a woman went to five locations and asked, "Could you pick up the five pages of Xerox for me?" In 60% of the situations, people did not respond to her request. Subsequently, the same test was carried out only with the justification "because I have so much work here that I will not be able to arrive on time" About 94% of the people responded promptly to the request! The next time you have to make a request, be sure to justify the reason!

5. Narrow Ties

Studies have proven that tightening bonds is one of the best techniques for gaining control over another person. The quickest way to have power over someone is to make them feel good in your presence, involving them emotionally. Researchers have discovered that engaging in some kind of activity with the other person generates an emotional connection. While you might find it complicated at first, it's quite simple. For example, you can share your songs as well as find which songs you like together. This will make them feel attached to you!

6. Listen More

If you are a very shy and introspective person, you will probably do this technique successfully. But if you are a more communicative person, do not worry. Studies have shown that people who listen more in the workplace or social gatherings assume a position of power over the others. If you are faced with a hard situation, try to control yourself and listen to everything others have to say. Expect them to ask you for your opinion. At times like this, all the caller's attention will come to you and it will be easier to have a pleasant conversation. This technique will increase your credibility and make your opinion the most considerable in any dialogue.

7. Tell the Truth

Did you know that little lies can end up hurting more than helping? Show the people around you that your life is not based on telling lies to please someone, but that you have a personality strong enough to speak the truth, even if it hurts. Be honest and you will have control of the situation much more easily than telling a lie and slipping afterward.

Use The Past to Influence a Person's Future

Do you realize how much the things you learned in childhood influence your present? Have you noticed that the way parents and educators created an individual's childhood affects their current talents and their fears and limitations? It is almost mathematical the result obtained nowadays. We can even use the equation: parents + education that we had = influence.

Want some practical examples to verify this reality? There is nothing better than the Numerological Challenges to show us the influence - positive or negative - of the way we were educated. The numbers in this position represent those fears that needed to be faced and overcome with our parents' help. It represents the kinds of attitudes and activities we fear most to develop and engage. Hence, the way parents and educators dealt with such difficulties when we were children may indicate whether we view them today with fear or as a differential in our behavior.

So it pays to do this dive into the past and understand the possible effects that the education you received has in your present.

Chapter 10: Brainwashing

Brainwashing as a manipulation technique is far more powerful than both mind control and hypnosis, but it also requires far more training and expertise to be used most efficiently. While many of the concepts used in hypnosis and mind control overlap with brainwashing, there are also new techniques made available to you when you learn about brainwashing.   Like hypnosis, brainwashing is a popular topic and plot device in many books, movies, and other media. Of course, as being the most powerful technique, brainwashing is also more high-profile than hypnosis and mind control. It has been used extensively in certain large-scale scenarios, including by certain governments, cults, corporations, etc.   While brainwashing has been known throughout history by many different names, including thought reform, thought control, coercive persuasion, and re-education for the sake of simplicity, this will only refer to it as brainwashing.

By learning more about what brainwashing is and how it works, you will not only have gained a valuable technique for manipulating other people, but you will also be able to more easily recognize when you are being brainwashed by another person or by an organization.

The History of Brainwashing

One of the most well-known portrayals of brainwashing on a massive scale in fiction is found in the book 1984, which was written by George Orwell in 1949.   In the book, a massive government entity maintains complete control over its citizens by creating propaganda, using surveillance to spy on people, rationing food, and even training people to use a different language.

There is no magical technology that allows the government to control its citizens' thoughts and actions directly. Still, through the laws it creates and how it enforces those laws, it can make its citizens think and act in only the ways that it wants them to.

Even though 1984 is a work of fiction, governments like the one described in the book have certainly existed in real life and continue to do so today. Of course, brainwashing has been used by other organizations than governments in its history, and different groups have used brainwashing successfully in different ways to further their goals.

While certain forms of brainwashing techniques have been in use for thousands of years, the public did not become aware of brainwashing on a large scale until the 1940s and the 1950s.

At that time, brainwashing was a major part of society in China under Mao Zedong, the Chairman of the Communist Party of China and China's leader overall. The term "brainwashing" comes from the Chinese phrase xǐnǎo, which translates to "wash brain" in English. Americans were not made aware of brainwashing as a phenomenon until after the Korean War had begun. During the war, American soldiers were captured as prisoners of war (POWs), and during their time spent in Chinese prison facilities, they were brainwashed by the Chinese government. The POWs that had been brainwashed were more likely to give over classified information to the Chinese and give false confessions, more willing to do what their captors wanted them to, and even defended the Chinese government's actions.

The United Nations commander at the time stated that "too familiar are the mind-annihilating methods of these Communists in forcing whatever words they want...The men themselves are not to be liable and they have my deepest compassion for having been used in this awful way." In other words, the Chinese were extremely skilled at brainwashing their victims, who would feel the effects of being brainwashed for years after it had been done to them. After American POWs were found to have been brainwashed, the United States Central Intelligence Agency (CIA) ran a series of experiments over twenty years that tested mind control and brainwashing capabilities, the most famous of these experiments being called Project MKUltra. To testing general brainwashing techniques, the CIA also experimented with drugs as a tool for manipulation and attempted to create a so-called truth serum that would be used for interrogation purposes.

From there, brainwashing took hold in the public's minds and began to play a large part in popular culture. Large audiences received stories involving brainwashing, and movies such as The Fearmakers, Toward the Unknown, The Bamboo Prison, The Rack, and The Manchurian Candidate were all inspired in some part by the experience of American POWs during the war or brainwashing in general. Starting in the late 1960s and extending through the mid-1970s, brainwashing as a concept was so deeply rooted in the public consciousness that it even seeped into the criminal justice system. Perhaps the most famous example is Patty Hearst, an heiress who was kidnapped and brainwashed by a terrorist group known as the Symbionese Liberation Army (SLA). She later joined the group as a member and was arrested during an attempted bank robbery.

Her trial was the first widely publicized instance of using brainwashing as a legal defense in court. While she was ultimately found guilty, the defense caused a renewal of interest and concern over brainwashing.

Since the 1960s, brainwashing has also been widely used in recruiting members to cults. The most well-known instance of brainwashing being used in cults is probably that of the Manson Family, founded in 1967 by Charles Manson. Manson was an extremely skilled manipulator, and successfully recruited nearly 100 people, mostly women, into his cult following. He had such a strong influence over them that he was able to convince them to commit several different crimes, from assault and robbery to mass murder. Nearly all cults use some form of brainwashing to influence potential recruits and convince them to join, from the most infamous to cults you have never heard of before. Some cults, such as Heaven's Gate and The People's Temple, used brainwashing to such a powerful effect that their followers were convinced to commit suicide.

Cults are especially important to study brainwashing because they demonstrate how far the power of brainwashing techniques can take people and are a good indicator of when things have gone too far. Suppose you are thinking of using brainwashing or any other manipulation on a person to make them inflict harm on themselves or anyone else. In that case, you should refrain from doing so and seek professional help for yourself.

But why is the history of brainwashing so important to learn about? After all, you are not a government entity such as the Communist Party of China, and you are hopefully not planning on dabbling in becoming a cult leader of any kind. Of course, there are valuable lessons to be learned from the history of brainwashing that you can apply to how you approach and implement brainwashing techniques in your own life. First of all, having a great understanding of brainwashing history should mean that you also have a good understanding of just how powerful brainwashing can be, even on the most unwilling targets. If American soldiers can be brainwashed into defending their captors, the country's enemies that they vowed to serve, then imagine what brainwashing can do for you if used correctly. Secondly, brainwashing history teaches the important lesson that anybody and everybody are susceptible to brainwashing techniques unlike mind control and hypnosis. If you focus on honing your talents and become a skilled enough manipulator, you can brainwash not just one person, but multiple people at a time into doing whatever it is that you want for them to do. The most talented manipulators can exert their influence over hundreds of people all at once, and every single one of their targets will be as thoroughly taught as the last one. This leads me into the final reason why the history of brainwashing is important to have at least some knowledge of because brainwashing is such a powerful and effective tool that can be used on so many people, it can be easy to take brainwashing too far, and force your targets into criminal or even life-threatening situations. By studying brainwashing history, you will know how horrible the effects of brainwashing can be for the target, the manipulator, and for anybody else who gets caught in between. While brainwashing as a tactic is not in and of itself harmful, when used with reckless abandon, things can quickly spiral out of control. As the manipulator, it is your responsibility to know when to stop before something terrible has occurred. Above all else, brainwashing history demonstrates the need to be safe, sensible, and responsible when using brainwashing techniques, as the consequences can be dire if brainwashing is used irresponsibly.

Chapter 11: 10 Steps of Brainwashing

Brainwashing phrases are mostly separate and can be generally divided into three levels. The first stage involves all the methods the abuser takes to tear down their prey; the second phase requires convincing the prey that there is a possibility of redemption; and lastly, the 3rd stage is where the target redeems itself and embraces his new self.

First Stage: Breaking the Target

Step 1: Identity Assaulting

To break down a predator's target, they may be the first target that makes the victim what they are: their ego or identity. Each human being has in his mind an idea of himself which is what they claim to be. This is the way they define themselves. Multiple identities are possible. You could be a mother and a career woman. You may be a smart businessman and an uncle. You may be a hard-fought student at the class. You just might be a Christian. You can choose between endless identities. That identity is your solution to the declaration tell me about yourself a little bit.

Suppose one day you wake up and someone advised you that you're not really what you believe you are. How do you manage to hear that? If this was deliberated in passing, you should possibly shrug it off and go on with your career. Or maybe you'd worry about it for a few hours or minutes, and maybe get frustrated for a bit, then push on. Now imagine someone comes to your home every minute of the day to remind you that you're not the guy you believe you are. How'd that help you feel? If it lasted through months or even weeks, then you will be out of your head by the end of it. You will be startled and left to question where to distinguish between fiction and fact.

If you'd thought about yourself as a great writer before, you'd start to doubt it. If you thought you were your children's biological father, you may start questioning him. If you've grown up thinking you're a real catholic, hearing daily contradictory reports would make you start thinking you might not be.

The first phase in the brainwashing cycle is when the entire dirty work starts taking hold. An individual who has planted the ugly seed of doubt in them is endangered to manipulation. We want to think the best of ourselves, as human beings. Also, we like having other people believe in us the best. Yes, some individuals may not care about someone else's validation and approval. That's admirable and we should all be working towards that. But at the last of the day, the guy who goes to bed thinking he is the worst of the bad periods of sleep more restlessly. Having high self-esteem and a strong sense of self, of course, saves you from the predators willing to attack you.

The result of the first phase of brainwashing is a completely-blown identity issue which the predator could prey on for the second step's purposes.

Step 2: Guilt Manipulation

Guilt, as it's been called, maybe a negative emotion, it is also a quite strong feeling. Guilt can start making you, as a person, promise things outside of your scope. Guilt will make you sit awake for hours wondering if you're such a bad human being because you're not. The human creatures around us are continually harnessing the strength of liability.

This is how the second phase of brainwashing tends to work: a brainwasher has indeed convinced its victim that they're not really what they've always assumed to be. Hence, the survivor is in a state of uncertainty because they try to address the issue of identification. Such that, if they aren't a decent guy, why are they then? The predator glides in at this point and begins to take them for their lives' entire sorrow trip. When you're uncertain who you are, it can be tempting to accept every falsehood you're getting fed up with about you. A brainwasher would also make a statement convincing their perpetrator that they are a nasty friend, irrespective of how this adverb is being used.

Steps 3 and 4: Personality-betrayal and breaking point

Even citizens themselves are intensely loyal. They're going to protect themselves and their behavior, and struggle to hear their words. Particularly the individuals who are afraid of speaking up for anyone also will speak up for themselves. A person having been brainwashed is the total opposite. Brainwashed people have no trouble rejecting themselves and anything else connected to them despite being continuously bombarded by signals about being the reverse about what they once considered themselves to be. This involves their family, associates, value framework, and all other relationships they might have that link them to the old identification that has been 'evaluated' by the brainwasher and found 'seriously missing.'

There are several reasons why a person who has been brainwashed can easily find himself in this step and cannot fight back. For beginners, they've already moved through the first 2 phases and come out in doubt and guilt, feeling drowning and disoriented. But frequently they don't have the strength to strike off. Remember that there is sometimes a risk of serious harm if conformance is not accomplished, so the goal may be too scared to contradict all the predator's replies.

Second Stage: Dangling a Salvation Carrot

Step 5: The Olive Branch

After the first 3 stages of brainwashing, a survivor of brainwashing sometimes feels so bad about themselves because they try to save themselves at whatever expense. The survivor is also in bad emotional health and has a weak self-image. Those who have forgotten their longtime sense of belonging and will clutch up on any straws offered to feel something again. At this stage, a victim becomes expected to experience a nervous collapse, and that is the signal for the attacker to leap in and deliver redemption.

The manipulator would also offer an olive branch after tearing down their objective for a long period so that the goal will slip into the pit of thinking there is hope at the last of a tunnel. An olive branch at this point could be something from a sweet word to a gift, or perhaps even some type of personal affection. This olive branch helps to demonstrate the goal that there is certain leniency to gain when they're on the right side of the manipulator. A manipulator is above all a 'normal guy' who wishes them the best. That is at least what they have learned since the start of brainwashing.

Step 6: Being Forced To Confess

Take into account: You have been confined for an amount of time to intense mental abuse by an individual. You have wasted your sense of belonging and feel confused and angry. You 're facing a psychotic collapse or already experienced one and can't make every part of your life head or tails. Since leaving the social network you have existed in solitary isolation and can't think of the last moment you had such a decent meal. Then, one day, this individual comes up at your door carrying a steaming coffee pot and freshly prepared muffins. They just say they want to chat. You are inviting them to your building. You just can't believe it. It's the only love you've been receiving in the longest period. What do you believe your former abuser will be reacting to this unusual kindness?

You'll experience a sense of sovereign debt more often than not. Human beings enjoy being kind enough to reciprocate that compassion. Whenever somebody does something good for you, then in exchange, it is natural and wants to do anything better. For a brainwashed human, the desire to pay back is much greater as they believe they still have to compensate for anything they are incorrect about. The brainwashed side, therefore, will be more than willing to offer away some type of kindness. This goodness would always come in the shape of a lie, in their troubled minds. The perpetrator would usually give the alternative of an apology as a means to get paid back.

Step 7: Guilt Channeling

A brainwashed survivor is frequently filled by so much crushing remorse that they still have no scope for any other feeling after weeks or months of becoming told they 're mistaken on anything. The goal has been swamped by so much abuser psychological torment they don't realize what we feel most bad for. The victim simply knows he's guilty of anything. In this misunderstanding, the manipulator glides in and persuades them that guilt is due to all the bad people they've believed in before. The predator, in other words, streams the guilt into the system of belief. The victim now begins to associate their beliefs with the guilt and the responsibility of dealing with the guilt. By fact, the abuser wants to help their prey continue to equate all the negative emotions of their history and let them think that if they select different values, there is a possibility to be rescued and feel stronger.

Step 8: Guilt Relief

The victim is beginning to feel a little relieved to recognize that he's just not deeply bad; perhaps, it is his perceptions that are wrong. He can be correct again, by detaching himself from his beliefs. He sheds his remorse by relinquishing anything related to his prejudices, even those nearest to him. He admits the mistakes of his previous ways and can embark on the current set of values that the brainwasher provides.

Third Stage: Reconstruction of a Brainwashed Self

Step 9: Harmony and Progress

At this stage in brainwashing, the target is keen to redeem itself and look very good in the brainwasher's eyes. Even so, they will start rebuilding a new identity based on the manipulator's offered belief system. After passing through the torture and suffering of the early phases of brainwashing, an offender is assured that only pain and guilt will come from their old belief system. They are glad to be rid of the former life and replaced with a new self that is their safe place from all their suffering.

Step 10: Rebirth and Final Confession

The survivor also experiences a sense of satisfaction upon embracing the current moral structure to be finished for their history and all of the resulting pain. Like the stereotypical last rope on a sinking ship, they must stick to their new identities as this is the only happiness they have experienced in a long period. At this stage, the brainwasher succeeded in obtaining a conversion, and might even be conducting a ritual to invite the latest conversion into the holy inner circle. It is typical for the majority of offenders to be separated from their families. They're going to get it in their heads that they're better individuals today and don't have to deal with their previous negative stuff.

Chapter 12: The Effects of Brainwashing on Individuals & Groups

The effects of brainwashing itself (and how effective it is a method of psychological control) have been called into question by different groups of researchers and experts who have spent years studying the American soldiers who returned to the United States after being released from the war camps, but were labeled as victims of brainwashing at the time of their return. They claimed that the ones they did speak to were most likely converted through the physical torture and neglect they underwent and not the actual brainwashing process. Their main reason for thinking this is that of the tens of thousands of prisoners put through brainwashing experiments, and less than two dozen fell under the process of brainwashing. However, these are those soldiers who decided to return to the United States, and not those who were so turned against the home country that they decided to remain in the land of their captors even after the war was over and everyone was released.

Cults around the world have played a large role in the continued interest of brainwashing and its effects. From the outside, it is easy to say that cults are bizarre and difficult to understand why anyone would want to get involved in one. Still, the brainwashing, manipulation, and other influential psychological control practices by the leaders or recruiters of these groups are some of the most practiced and well-tested agents and manipulators in human culture. They accomplish this by targeting people who are most open to influence, making them special and part of a community and then convincing them through fake friendship or understanding that what they are doing or standing for is genuinely right and good.

Successful brainwashing can have several effects on individuals and groups of people in the long run. Some of the most common side effects that can be eased or reversed through a process of un-brainwashing (more commonly known as deprogramming) include:

- **Shattered sense of confidence**

This can often lead to a series of painful and damaging decisions after the fact such as dependence on alcohol or the use of stronger drugs

- **Inability to trust people**

From every random encounter to those they love with all their heart, people who have survived the brainwashing process (successful or otherwise) tend to retreat into themselves, unsure of how to trust people they are surrounded by after their ordeal

- **They see everything as a test**

A lot of life loses its excitement after a brainwashing process. The victim rarely has any interest in events or activities they once enjoyed, they have lost their drive and enthusiasm for the future

Each time they are offered an opportunity or invited to join in on a task, they hesitate and make sure to pull apart and analyze every detail before even thinking about whether or not it is something they want to take part in

How to Protect Yourself from Becoming the Target of Malevolent Brainwashing Techniques

Who is most susceptible to brainwashing techniques? Who is the most likely to become a victim of those seeking to improve their standing or just tear down others by convincing people to change their view of the world (sometimes a complete flip)?

One of the most common reasons people get drawn into cults or the control of a manipulative agent is that they have no idea what brainwashing looks like or what kinds of warning signs to look for. The first way to protect yourself from falling prey to these types of psychological predators is to recognize the traits they look for in potential targets:

· Loners who have never found their place, but have not given up on finding where they belong or who they fit in with

This is one reason those runaway teenagers are often targeted by brainwashing cults and similar groups. They have not yet developed the emotional maturity or life experience to realize they are being taken advantage of in most cases.

· They do not have anyone to stand up for them

This could be because they are anti-social by nature, but it is more likely because they are too stubborn to take the advice of others and have a tendency to get defensive when they are told what to do or that they should be more careful

· They are searching for answers or a purpose

This is when potential targets are drawn in by friends, family members, mentors or others that they know or have come to respect and trust. In cases like these, the agent uses their familiarity with the target and their knowledge of how they see the world to gain control of them

Providing their target with a sense of duty to get them on board with the brainwashing process is the first step that is then followed by inspiring feelings of guilt and disappointment in the target when they have hesitations or fail at their assigned task

No one thinks they are susceptible to brainwashing. The concept itself conjures images of malnourished prisoners forced to watch propaganda videos until they accept them as truth and captured spies being injected with clear liquids that alter their mental state to change their reality by chemical means. However, brainwashing is not always as dramatic but can still be as harmful and dangerous. Once a person has determined whether or not they have the potential to become a victim, the next step is to look for warning signs that brainwashing is happening around you. Some of the most notable and widely established include:

- Unfamiliar, confusing and often increasing sense of fear connected to the world outside of their home or wherever they are currently living
- Constant feeling of inadequacy even when they know they have done their absolute best
- Feelings of mistrust and struggles with anxiety attacks over not impossible, but often improbable events like natural disasters striking out of nowhere, the fear of terrorist attacks at each place they visit from public restrooms in their local grocery store to the sidewalk corner across from their living quarters
- Abandonment of communication devices (no cell phone or social media allowed) and disconnect from people they are usually social with

These warning signs will be reinforced, promoted and even introduced if they do not develop on their own by the people doing the brainwashing. Any time you feel these feelings, particularly if you are experiencing multiple signs at once, look at the actions and behaviors of the people you consider your friends, your partners, and even your superiors. If they make the feelings worse through the things they do or say or mock you for thinking something is wrong, they may be running a brainwashing process. From here, the next step is the most difficult because it involves either denying what you are suspecting as just your imagination or that you are just going through a bad time, confronting the person about your suspicions (although this rarely leads to any kind of resolution, giving the agent in question only more opportunity to manipulate your emotions and feelings to whatever they want you to believe, most likely through guilt or through reminding you of your connection, or by removing yourself from the situation and severing ties permanently o until you have a better grip on your mental state).

Whether brushed off as fiction in favor of more solid mind control methods like physical pain and health neglecting or embraced as worrisome and complex method of psychological manipulation, brainwashing still has a lot to offer in terms of how the human mind works, how different people react in different situations and just how confident people can be in who they are and what they believe in. There is no limit of studying going on around the world and, certainly, experts on the subject have only just begun to peel away the layer of intricacy involved in the field.